A DEEPER UNDERSTANDING...

For the bereaved, and anyone who is or has been touched by bereavement.

A chance to understand from first hand experience what it is like to go through bereavement and grief.

Copyright : Colin Boynton ~
Widowed 23rd September 2017 after 30 happy years with a wonderful husband and partner.

ISBN : 978 - 0 - 9559931 - 9 - 0

Introduction :

Bereavement is very real, but unfortunately not always recognized or seen as such. It is a very serious issue that needs treating as such – with HELP, LOVE, CARING & SUPPORT.

A person dealing with bereavement will get through it – but dealing with it alone and coming up against obstacles can make the journey harder and longer than necessary.

PLEASE – REMEMBER TO SHOW SOME COMPASSION, LOVE AND SUPPORT TO SOMEONE WHO IS BEREAVED BECAUSE ONE DAY IT COULD BE YOU IN THE SAME PLACE!

Angels.

When the rain falls from the sky
Is that when the angels cry?
Do they cry for what we do?
Do they cry for me and you?
When they smile do we see,
Their light shine down on you and me?
Are they happy are they bright?
Do they laugh with pure delight?
Watching us both night and day,
Hearing everything we say,
Watching over me and you,
Guarding us in all we do.
Thank the angels every day
For guarding us in their own way,
Thank the angels every night
For keeping us within their sight.

THERE IS NO GREATER POWER THAN THE POWER OF LOVE!

January 6th 2017 was the day I was given news I never expected to hear, or ever wanted to really hear. Sat having lunch that day there was a knock on the door. I opened it to find a policeman stood there, looking for me.

I invited him inside and I sat down wondering what the visit was about.

He then announced to me that my Brother had been found dead. My immediate reaction was total denial and disbelief, so he repeated what he had just told me. I went straight in to shock and never heard the rest of what he said to me or my husband. My Brother had only just turned 53 years old two weeks before, and he had been over visiting and celebrating with us.

9 months later while still getting over the death of my Brother, my husband went in to hospital. While there he was diagnosed with cancer and we were told that there was no treatment. It was explained at the time that we could expect between two and five years, and after two weeks in hospital my husband returned home and we started making plans of things we would do in the time we had left. After less than a week at home my husband was rushed back in to hospital. Within a few hours, once again I was confronted by the news I neither expected nor wanted to hear, my beloved

Husband and Partner for 30 years had died just a few minutes before I had got back to hospital to see him.

Within the space of less than a year, I had lost the two most important people in my life!

The following tries to explain a little of what I went through next, and how I dealt with it. Hopefully it will help you deal with a similar situation when you become confronted by it.

For most people the closest they will come to real bereavement will be when they lose their parents, a brother, a sister, an aunt or uncle, a treasured pet or a close friend - I've been through all that. But there is nothing comes close to losing your Partner, be it husband or wife – no matter how long you have been together – as childhood sweethearts or for just a year or so. It really doesn't matter, you shared your life with that someone special, you spent precious moments together, you will have been through good times and bad times, you will have helped each other along the way.

There are memories you created together. Your loved one became part of you as time progressed and no matter how often or how much or little you may have tried talking about the inevitable, you will never be fully prepared for what is to come.

For some it strikes suddenly without warning and for others it will have taken time in arriving, even though they knew it would not be too far away for them. Whatever the circumstances are, there is nothing at all that can prepare the one's left behind, for what is about to hit them, and when it does hit, it hits so hard it literally can knock you off your feet!

TEAR STAINS.

Tear stains on my pillow
I cry each night for you,
For all that's left are memories
Of things we used to do.
A kiss to make me better,
A smile to make me laugh,
And memories held dear to me
Within a photograph.
Thank you for the love you gave,
And all the caring too,
I'm really glad I had the chance
To say - My Dear

-

"I Love You"

The first thing you feel when you lose someone is disbelief and shock. You feel that some huge mistake has been made and that the news you have just been given must be incorrect. You deny that it could ever have happened, you try to tell yourself that the words that you have just heard were not meant for your ears but for someone else – but there is no someone else there with you, you are alone.

...then there are the guilt feelings...
... the feelings of being left alone...
... and feeling lost.

You then keep asking yourself if there was more that you could have done to prevent what has happened from happening. You ask yourself and others "Did I do enough?" Even though you know that there was nothing more anybody could have done. You question why your loved one has left you alone ...

...and also there is the grief and sorrow that is so painful. The hurt is almost unbelievable. The tears flow long and hard and seem never ending - but you need to let them out and you need to let out your grief. You cannot even begin to describe the pain that you feel as it is a pain like you have never felt before in your life.
It doesn't matter how much you explain to people, and how often you tell them, they will never really understand how much your grief hurts when you have lost the one you love and have loved for so long. And the pain goes on for such a long time.

When you lose that one person who you loved dearly, spent your life with, cared for, shared all with, then you are left with such a large gap, a hole in your life, that bereavement becomes very real to you. You have a huge dark gaping hole inside that you feel can never be filled. You start to feel that you cannot go on, that it is not worth going on. You lose your sense of "Purpose" in life. You start to lose all faith and have little hope, the darkness descends upon you and you start to stumble around, hands reaching out looking for the way forward, but you just cannot find it.

You cannot prepare for it no matter how the end comes, even if you have a warning and you know it is coming. You cannot prepare for or imagine the grief that will hit you and at times become all consuming. You cannot imagine the pain and hurting inside which engulfs you and seems at times never ending. You cannot even imagine the amount of tears you will shed, even when you think there are no more tears left within, there are more keep flowing down your cheeks, and each tear that falls is filled with the pain and the hurting – an unimaginable pain, a pain that is hard to describe because you have never experienced anything like it before. You cannot run from it and you cannot hide from it, the best you can do is to let it take its course. But at times like this you need love and support from those around you, and, although they may not understand how you are feeling they need to be patient and supportive.

SHOW THE WORLD.

YOU CANNOT RUN
YOU CANNOT HIDE
FROM THE DEMONS
HID INSIDE
YOU MAY NOT LIKE
THE THINGS YOU SEE
THEY'RE STILL A PART
OF YOU OR ME
YOU MAY NOT LIKE
THE THINGS YOU HEAR
ECHO SOUNDS
WITHIN YOUR EAR
YOU SAY THE THINGS
YOU HAVE TO SAY
TO GET YOU THROUGH
FROM DAY TO DAY
YOU FIND THE COURAGE
LOSE THE FEAR
TAKE WHAT'S YOURS
AND HOLD IT NEAR
SO DO NOT RUN
STAND PROUD AND TALL
AND SHOW THE WORLD
YOU HAVE IT ALL.

You need time too. Time to find yourself - you certainly do not need people telling how you should be living your life now, what you should and should not be doing. These are things that only you can decide upon. You will know whether you are ready for something or not. And it is no good people saying "Your loved one would have wanted you to do this" or "Your loved one would not want you to do that" Only you know these things, after all, you were the person who lived with your loved one, you are the person who shared a life together with your loved one – not those people telling you what you should and shouldn't do. In your own time you will become ready to venture out and do things – but do them for yourself, not to please others – **You are the person who is going through this bereavement, not them.** If you cannot face something or handle something, it is no use trying to do them just to please others, please yourself first, because during this period **You** are the most important person there is.

NEVER FORGET

HOW TO SMILE

AND

NEVER FORGET

HOW TO LAUGH

You cannot simply "Pull yourself together" – As people will tell you to do.
As the bereaved person, your whole world has been torn apart and turned upside down. You have to learn to live all over again, but this time you have to do it alone, without your chosen partner beside you and helping you. And like when you first started to learn how to live as a growing young person, you once again have to take it slowly, one step at a time, day by day, building up confidence and building new bridges to where you want to be, and what will be your new life. You have to learn to cope with what life will throw your way, and the obstacles that life and people will put in your way.

We are not taught how to deal with bereavement, we are not taught how to handle people who are going through bereavement. Instead we tend to turn away from the bereaved, just when they need help the most. People on the outside need as much strength as those going through bereavement to be able to deal with such a huge emotional event in life.

Never ignore the bereaved person when you see them on the street. You may find it awkward and difficult, but it really hurts when people you know start to ignore you just because they are unsure how to handle you. It is much better for you to say to the bereaved "Hello, how are you today?" and cause tears, than to ignore them. At least the bereaved knows you care about them and what they are going through.

All we actually need, is to be greeted with a pleasant "Hello!" that is enough to prevent us from feeling left out and unwanted in our hours of need.

FREE TO BE

I SEE THE TEARS BEHIND YOUR EYES
YOU DO NOT LET THEM GO
THE SMILE YOU HAVE UPON YOUR FACE
IS FALSE, OF THAT I KNOW
YOU HOLD BACK YOUR EMOTIONS
YOU KEEP THEM HID AWAY
AND ONLY LET YOUR FEELINGS OUT
AT CLOSING OF THE DAY
YOU DO NOT SHARE THEM WITH US
AFRAID THAT WE MIGHT SEE
JUST WHAT IS GOING THROUGH YOUR MIND
BE BRAVE AND LET THEM BE
DO NOT EVER WORRY
WHAT OTHERS THINK OF YOU
BE YOURSELF THE BEST YOU CAN
AND DO WHAT YOU MUST DO
YOU ARE YOU AND STAY THAT WAY
JUST AS I AM ME
NO MATTER WHAT YOU HAVE TO DO
LIVE YOUR LIFE BE FREE.

Are you the kind of person who says "Just pick up the phone – you know where we are"?

There are things that become very difficult to do, and one of those is to simply pick up the telephone to speak to someone about how you are feeling. That telephone becomes the heaviest object at hand. Why not pick that phone up yourselves if you really mean it, phone the person who is bereaved, let them hear a human voice, show you care, show you really mean what you say.

For the Bereaved there is also the fear that when they try to make that phone call they will either get no response or the response they get is not one that they can easily handle – "I'm sorry I'm too busy just now" or "Can you call back later?"

Do not say you will be there for someone and will help if they need it, if you know down inside you will not be able to cope with it. It causes more distress to the bereaved when you turn them away in their darkest hours of need, just say you are "Sorry, but as much as I would like to help, I just don't feel I have the strength at this moment in time" They will understand and accept that. There is nothing wrong with being open and honest about it.

Sometimes all you want and need is a hug. Someone to put their arms around you and hold you for a couple of minutes and reassure you that everything will be alright. You do not need to do it for long, just a few minutes can make all the difference.

At special times of the year like Christmas when going through bereavement, it would be more thoughtful and beneficial if people sent blank cards and wrote inside "Thinking Of You" rather than sending a card saying "Merry Christmas" or "Happy Christmas" as it will be neither when going through your first Christmas without the one you Love. It will even be hard as each Christmas comes around bringing memories of happy times you used to spend together.

"Be Kind To Yourself!" is something I was told time and time again, yet when I asked for an explanation, few people could actually tell me what they meant until one day it was told to me in very simple terms. An example being that some days you will find that you have no motivation at all and all you will want to do is sit around doing nothing, and not be disturbed. Well do it!!! Don't feel guilty. You may feel like just dropping everything and going out but with no place to go and no agenda. Well do it! Don't feel guilty about it. If some days all you feel like doing is staying in bed and sleeping. Well do it! Just learn to listen to what your body and mind tells you. It knows what you want, no one else can tell you. BE KIND TO YOURSELF.

If there is one thing I have learnt in the past months is that, the majority of people are self centered and selfish thinking only of themselves. Only saying they care, to make themselves both look and feel good but with no real truth, feeling or meaning behind what they actually say.

It can be amazing what will set the tears flowing during the period of bereavement, a piece of music, a picture, something you read in a book or newspaper or even coming across something unexpected. It really doesn't matter what it might be, but you just have to let the emotions out, and it really does not matter where you are when it happens, and it does not matter who sees you, there is no reason to feel ashamed or worried if you have to cry when out in public. I have even done it when out doing the weekly shopping – it really does not matter at all, as long as you let it out.

LITTLE KNOCKS CAN SOMETIMES HURT THE MOST.

Life becomes an emotional rollercoaster during bereavement, some days you can feel very happy and be getting on with life as if the whole bereavement process was over, then other days you feel so sad and depressed, that you begin to wonder if the process will ever end, it just feels like it is going on week after week without an end in sight.

On good days you want to get out into the world and do as much as possible to start living again but on the bad days, some people have no motivation to move and just sit around staring at four walls from morning until night, others will get out and about but with no purpose behind it, not knowing what they are doing or where they are going, they just need to escape the prison of the four walls.

Another problem that can strike when going through bereavement is anxiety and panic attacks. Try not let yourself be forced into doing something you feel uncomfortable with which might cause you anxiety, if you don't feel strong enough to handle doing something, just say "No!" to it. Nothing is that important that you must do it. You are more important than trivial matters.

Another way that you can "Be Kind to yourself" can just be treating yourself to something nice, or making a special meal. Soaking in a hot bath for a while, whatever it is I think is up to you. Just do something that actually makes you happy and feel good, no matter how big or small it might be, just do it.

Bereavement counselling is good but can be physically and emotionally tiring. Memories surface that you try hard to forget – memories that bring pain and sorrow and you find really hard to handle, but there are also the memories that also bring tears, but are tears of joy, but in the end whichever type of memory is brought out and brings tears, it is very emotionally tiring.
The counselling also helps you realise that although you are grieving for a lost love, it is

fine to laugh, to cry and to try and put your life back together and start to live again. There is no disrespect for the departed – the memories you have prove that, and you start to realise that you cannot live in memories alone, you need to live now and you need to love yourself and take care of yourself as you have your future still to come.

And although we have our memories, they can never take the place of our lost loves.

Memories will forever be SECOND BEST

SECOND BEST

PEOPLE SAY I SHOULD BE HAPPY
WITH MY MEMORIES
THEY SAY I SHOULD BE GRATEFUL
FOR ALL MY "USED TO BE'S"
BUT YOU CANNOT HOLD A MEMORY
AND HUG IT CLOSE AND TIGHT
YOU CANNOT KISS A MEMORY
TO WISH IT A GOODNIGHT
YOU CANNOT LISTEN TO ITS HEART
WHILE RESTING ON ITS CHEST
ALL THE MEMORIES THAT YOU HAVE
ARE ONLY SECOND BEST
SECOND TO THE ONE YOU LOVED
FOR ALL THOSE MANY YEARS
AND UNLIKE ALL THOSE MEMORIES
NEVER BROUGHT YOU TEARS.

Another thing that takes some getting used to, is, the forgetfulness, the lack of concentration, the lack of motivation and the poor memory.

One thing that does not help all of these things, is how easy it is to get distracted from what you are doing.

You easily forget things – either things that need doing or you may be in the middle of doing something, get distracted and forget all about what you were doing.

You may also set out to do something and find you cannot concentrate long enough to complete the task at hand, or you may find that you simply do not have the motivation at all to do anything.

You will find "NEW" things easier to handle than old things as they don't hold memories of your lost loved one.

You set out to do some things that are "Old and Familiar" but find you just simply cannot do them, you might get anxiety attacks or panic attacks or just break down in tears, unable to deal with that something which might be so familiar to you, yet you set out to do something which you have never done before and find it the easiest thing for you to do.

The reason behind how you react to these things is, old and familiar things have memories attached to them, even if your lost one did not do something with you, you still have memories of setting out, doing whatever it is you were doing and then returning home to your loved one after doing something. When you set out to do something that is completely new to you, you have NO memories attached making it much easier to deal with.

We really need to talk about what has happened, about our loved ones and about our loss and how we are feeling – both the bereaved and those looking on do need to spend time talking, expressing themselves and discussing everything, hiding from it and ignoring it only makes it harder later on to deal with what has happened.
Be free, express yourselves and be friends with yourselves.

There is no time limit on how long bereavement will last, everyone is different and everyone will take different amounts of time. You will have good days and bad days trying to understand what has happened. You will have questions to ask, and sometimes no one has the answer that you are looking for. As time passes you may wonder how long the grief will last, will it always hurt as much as it does now or will it ease.

TIME – that's all we have and all we need, time to recover, time to learn to live with what has happened, but because everybody is different and we all have different circumstances that length of time will be different – but the main thing is however long it takes – it isn't wrong or right – you just take the time you need, and one day you will realise that it is Time To Move On.

Put things down in writing – it's very helpful. Whether it is on paper, on your computer, on social media, you will always feel better

if you put things down in writing. Express yourself freely and as much as you want, and if you put it down on paper, you do not have to keep it. It can be for your eyes only and destroyed at a later date.
Only you yourself, going through bereavement will know what is the right thing and what is the wrong thing to do. Listen to your heart. People like to give good advice, but unless they have been through what you are going through, it may be the wrong advice they give you and may cause more grief and upset.

It doesn't matter how much you try to explain to people, and how often you tell them, they will never really understand how much your grief hurts when you have lost the one you love and have loved for so long. And the pain goes on for such a long time.

Just work through things in your own way, it is your grief and your bereavement not someone else's. Every person is different and will deal with things in a different way, the one thing that will remain constant is to just BE YOURSELF and not what someone says you should be.

It does not matter how much time passes by, and not matter what some people may say to you, yes life does go on, but you cannot simply "Get Over It!" You have to learn how to live with what has happened, and that is going to take time.

THE GRIEF IS YOURS
AND YOURS ALONE.
TIME IS YOURS AND
YOURS ALONE
TAKE WHATEVER TIME
YOU NEED –
YOU DO NOT HAVE TO
RUSH IT

After the bereavement and the grief comes the loneliness. The realization that there is no longer someone there at your side, someone to talk to, someone to laugh with and someone to simply share life with. Going places no longer has the same meaning once you are left on your own. Driving in the car with no one beside you suddenly becomes a lonely experience.

This is the time more than ever that you need to have friends around – people who can and will support you. Without these people life can become very difficult, and moving on can become an extremely hard task to do.

During the whole process of bereavement a person needs to be allowed the time to have plenty of rest and recouperation, it is a most physically and mentally tiring process to go through, and, without that rest a person will, if not careful, have a serious breakdown adding more problems to the problems already being dealt with.

There is also a lot of "Rebuilding" to be done. Home life, Social life, and Work life. All of these things change in such a large way and need time to be worked on and worked out.
And as strange as it may sound, you also have to learn how to communicate with people again. People also need to learn how to communicate with the bereaved person. Things will be different, things will have changed, not just for the short term, but FOREVER.

I found I had to deal with many different companies and organizations during my period of bereavement. Most of these were very understanding and helpful. But I suggest that if you have to deal with anyone – GET ASSISTANCE!!! Not everyone recognises bereavement as a serious problem and it can be difficult to get them to understand that someone has died and what it is like for you.

Eventually comes the start of "Acceptance" This is not an easy thing at all and can bring about as much pain and as many tears as the original bereavement.
Acceptance that :

1) Your loved one is no longer beside you
2) There will forever be an empty place at the table
3) Whenever you go out alone, there will no longer be that someone waiting for you to get home to again
4) You are now on your own

"I BELIEVE IN ME!"

THOUGHTS FOR CONFIDENCE AND INSPIRATION

The following few phrases are what I came up with in the weeks and months after being bereaved and when my confidence was at its lowest point. Writing these down and then reading them back at times reminded me that there was hope and that I would one day be back and on top and living my life again – and I now I am.

**I CAN BE WHAT I WANT
DO WHAT I WANT
AND HAVE WHAT I WANT
BECAUSE I BELIEVE IN ME!**

**I AM SO GRATEFUL FOR MY LIFE, THE WONDERFUL THINGS I HAVE IN IT – NICE CLOTHES TO WEAR, GOOD FOOD TO EAT, A LOVELY COMFORTABLE HOME, NICE THINGS ABOUT ME, MY FREEDOM TO DO WHAT I WANT AND BE WHAT I WANT.
I AM SO GRATEFUL FOR MY LIFE
AND I AM SO
VERY HAPPY!!!**

I CAN HOLD MY HEAD UP HIGH
I CAN STAND PROUD AND TALL
I CAN WALK WITH A SPRING IN MY STEP
BECAUSE –
I BELIEVE IN ME!

I AM STRONG –
NOW
WATCH ME GROW
BECAUSE
I BELIEVE IN ME!

I DON'T NEED WINGS TO FLY!

I AM HAPPY AND I LIKE ME!

FROM THE COCOON OF SADNESS
AND DESPAIR
EMERGES
THE BUTTERFLY OF HAPPINESS AND LIFE!

AS LONG AS I LOVE MYSELF
THAT IS ALL THAT MATTERS…
THE REST WILL FOLLOW ON

NOW MY SUN HAS STARTED SHINING –
NOTHING CAN STOP ME FROM GROWING
BIG AND STRONG.

NEVER FORGET HOW TO SMILE
AND
NEVER FORGET HOW TO LAUGH

SSHHH I CAN HEAR SINGING
OH!
IT'S ME!
IT'S MY HEART!!
AND I'M HAPPY!!!

WHO SAY'S I CANNOT –
AND WHY SHOULDN'T I?

IF I CAN'T BE TRUE TO MYSELF
THEN
WHO CAN I BE TRUE TO?

THE DOOR TO MY WORLD IS ALWAYS OPEN
BUT –
MESS ME AROUND AND I'LL CLOSE IT TO
YOU!

I'M GOING TO LIVE MY LIFE THE WAY I WANT.
IT DOESN'T MATTER WHAT PEOPLE THINK AS LONG AS I AM HAPPY – AND I AM!

FINALLY-

THERE IS NO GREATER POWER THAN THE POWER OF LOVE!

FINALLY - FREEDOM

You have Freedom.
Freedom to make choices.
Freedom to do whatever you want whenever you want — no matter how hard that freedom is to accept.
You Now Have FREEDOM.

THE COURAGE YOU DON'T LACK

FACE THE WORLD AND FACE YOUR FEARS
THERE MIGHT BE WORSE TO COME
TAKE YOUR HEART, TAKE YOUR MIND
JUST DO WHAT MUST BE DONE
TAKE A STEP AND THEN ONE MORE
AS HARD AS IT MAY BE
NO ONE'S REALLY WATCHING YOU
WELL WHO CARES WHAT THEY SEE
HAVE THEY FACED THE SAME FEARS?
AND BEEN THERE ALL ALONE
WALKING IN THE DARKNESS
AND FACING THE UNKNOWN
IT MAY TAKE LOTS OF COURAGE
IT'S SOMETHING YOU DON'T LACK
JUST FACE TOWARD THE FUTURE
MAKE SURE YOU DON'T LOOK BACK
AND AS YOU MAKE THAT FIRST STEP
THE NEXT ONE'S NOT SO BAD
ALTHOUGH YOU MOVE ON SLOWLY
YOU'LL FIND IT MAKES YOU GLAD
GLAD YOU MADE THE EFFORT -

GLAD YOU TOOK A CHANCE -

GLAD THAT YOU'RE BACK LIVING -

AND JOINING IN LIFE'S DANCE.

AND FINALLY...

"THE FUTURE HOLDS OUR FATE IN ITS HANDS"

I HOPE THIS LITTLE BOOK WILL BECOME A USEFUL GUIDE TO ALL WHO PICK IT UP AND READ IT.

IT HAS BEEN WRITTEN WITH THE INTENTION OF SHOWING THE WORLD WHAT I WENT THROUGH WITH BEREAVEMENT, AND TO HOPEFULLY HELP AS OTHERS DEAL WITH THE SAME, AND ALSO TO HELP THOSE WHO WANT TO BE THERE FOR THE BEREAVED PERSON.

NOT EVERYBODY IS THE SAME AND SOME PEOPLE GET THROUGH THINGS AT A MUCH FASTER PACE, BUT EACH AND EVERY PERSON HAS SOMETHING IN COMMON, AND IF NOT NOW, WILL HAVE AT SOME POINT IN THEIR LIVES.

BY THE END OF THE FIRST YEAR AFTER BEREAVEMENT, I BEGAN TO REALIZE THAT I WAS BECOMING A RECLUSE. I DIDN'T WANT TO LEAVE THE HOUSE, EXCEPT TO DO THE WEEKLY SHOPPING. I ALSO NEITHER KNEW HOW, NOR WANTED TO, MIX AND SOCIALISE WITH PEOPLE. I WAS SLOWLY CLOSING MYSELF OFF FROM THE OUTSIDE WORLD. I WAS GETTING INTO A SITUATION WHERE I NO LONGER CARED OR BOTHERED. NOTHING SEEMED TO MATTER ANY MORE. BEING ALONE NOW, NO LONGER SEEMED A PROBLEM. I WAS FEEDING MYSELF – IN A WAY, I WAS LOOKING AFTER THE DOG BETTER

THAN I WAS LOOKING AFTER MYSELF. I WAS JUST - SURVIVING.

BUT THEN SOMETHING CHANGED. I MET NEW FRIENDS WHO WANTED TO TALK WITH ME, AND WANTED ME AROUND. I BEGAN DOING SOME VOLUNTARY WORK WHICH GAVE ME BACK SOME OF THE SELF RESPECT I HAD LOST ALONG THE WAY.

I STARTED TO FEEL THAT I WANTED TO GET OUT AND START LIVING AGAIN – DOING THINGS THAT MADE ME FEEL GOOD ABOUT MYSELF. I ALSO FOUND MYSELF MAKING PLANS FOR THE FUTURE. A WEIGHT WAS BEING LIFTED FROM MY SHOULDERS AND I WAS NOW FINDING REASONS TO LIVE. AND ALL BECAUSE I HAD FOUND NEW

FRIENDS, INTRODUCED NEW PEOPLE INTO MY LIFE, WHO IN TURN WERE INTRODUCING ME TO THEIR FRIENDS. I WAS BACK OUT IN THE WORLD ONCE AGAIN WITH A SOCIAL LIFE.

SO, I KNEW I STILL HAD A LONG WAY TO GO AS I REBUILT MY LIFE, BUT I WAS NOW DOING IT, SLOWLY DAY BY DAY AND WEEK BY WEEK. I ACCEPTED THAT IT WAS GOING TO TAKE SOME TIME. I STILL HAD THOSE "FIRSTS" TO GET THROUGH, BUT I KNEW NOW THAT I WAS GETTING STRONGER AND WOULD BE ABLE TO GET THROUGH, EVEN THOUGH THERE WOULD BE MANY MORE TEARS TO SHED AND MORE PAIN TO BEAR IN MY HEART.

FOR THOSE OF YOU WHO ARE GOING THROUGH THE PROCESS OF BEREAVEMENT

MY THOUGHTS AND PRAYERS GO OUT TO YOU AND MAY YOU FIND PEACE AND HAPPINESS AGAIN ONE DAY.

I DEDICATE THIS BOOK TO ASHGATE HOSPICE AND EVERYONE WHO WORKS THERE. WITHOUT THEIR HELP LOVE AND SUPPORT I WOULD NOT HAVE GOT THROUGH THE DARKEST AND HARDEST DAYS IN MY LIFE THAT I HAVE EVER EXPERIENCED. ASHGATE HOSPICE - AN AMAZING PLACE WITH TRULY AMAZING PEOPLE GIVING THEIR TIME TO SUPPORT OTHERS WHO ARE IN NEED.

THANK -YOU!

TOGETHER.

WE'RE STANDING HERE UPON THE EDGE
LOOKING OUT AT LIFE
SOME WITHOUT A HUSBAND
AND SOME WITHOUT A WIFE
OUR GRIEF IS SAILING CLOSE TO SHORE
BUT DRIFTING FURTHER ON
SOME DAYS WE DO NOT SEE IT
YET KNOW IT HASN'T GONE.
WE WALK ALONG THE EDGE OF LIFE
FEELING ALL ALONE
LOOKING FOR THE LOST SOUL
OF SOMEONE WE HAD KNOWN
WE DO NOT SEE THE OTHERS
WHO WALK THE PATH AS WELL
WE'RE BLINDED BY THE TEARS WE SHED
OUR LIFE AN EMPTY SHELL
THEN SOMEONE HOLDS A HAND OUT
SOMEONE WE DON'T KNOW
WE GRASP THE HAND IN FAITH AND HOPE
OUR STRENGTH BEGINS TO GROW
AND WITH OUR STRENGTH OUR COURAGE GROWS
WE START TO MAKE NEW FRIENDS
WE START TO FEEL NEW HAPPINESS
THOUGH SORROW NEVER ENDS
AND NOW WE STAND TOGETHER
LOOKING OUT AT LIFE
ONE WAS ONCE A HUSBAND
AND ONE WAS ONCE A WIFE
BUT NOW WE HAVE NEW FRIENDSHIP
WITH PEOPLE WHO CAN SHARE
PEOPLE BROUGHT TOGETHER
WHO SHOW THEY REALLY CARE
ALL GOING THROUGH THE SAME THINGS
WHILE LIVING DAY TO DAY
SUPPORTING ONE ANOTHER
WHILST GOING ON OUR WAY.

I LEAVE THE NEXT FEW PAGES BLANK SO THAT YOU CAN MAKE YOUR OWN NOTES AS YOU GO ON YOUR JOURNEY. YOU MAY WANT TO SHARE THESE NOTES WITH OTHERS OR THEY MIGHT BE FOR YOUR EYES ONLY :

www.ingramcontent.com/pod-product-compliance
Lightning Source LLC
Chambersburg PA
CBHW071756040426
42446CB00012B/2590